Grandpa's New Scooter

Dana   Grandpa

Written by Jack Gabolinscy
Illustrated by Philip Webb

My dad and I visited Grandpa last weekend. He was sitting at the table with his walking stick and a long face.

"What's the matter?" my dad asked Grandpa. "You don't look very happy."

"I'm not," said Grandpa. "I'm very unhappy. My legs are getting old and tired. I can't visit my friends any more."

"Oh!" said Dad. "That is really sad."

"You can borrow my scooter, Grandpa," I said.

3

Grandpa looked at me.
"Thank you, Dana," he said.
"You are very kind, but I'm going to
buy my own scooter. I'm going to
get a three-wheeled scooter with a
battery. Then I will be able to visit
my friends and buy my groceries."

STANDARD

LUXURY

SUPER DELUX

5

A few days later, Dad and I went back to see Grandpa's new scooter. It was bright red, with a long black seat and a little horn that beeped loudly. It even had a basket to carry groceries.

It's cool!

"Wow!" I said. "What a cool scooter!"

"No, it's not!" said Grandpa. "It doesn't go fast enough. A snail with a broken leg could go faster than this scooter."

"You don't want to go fast," said Dad. "You don't want it to be like a motorbike."

7

Grandpa smiled. He looked at me. "Yes, I do," he said. "I want a scooter that roars like thunder and streaks like a fireball through space!"

"You can't go too fast," I said. "The police will follow you to make sure you don't speed."

"But I want the fastest scooter in the world!" said Grandpa.

This morning, I went to see Grandpa again.

"I've fixed up my scooter," he said. "I'm going for a ride. Do you want to come?"

"OK, Grandpa," I said. "Will it be strong enough for me, too?"

"I've made some changes. This scooter is strong enough for ten people now," said Grandpa.

He opened the garage door. There was his shiny red scooter with a new name painted like a flash of fire on the side.

"I've changed the battery, too," he said. "The old one wasn't strong enough, so I put two big ones in."

handlebars

mag wheels

chrome exhaust

paint

spoiler

13

Grandpa got on the scooter and pushed the starter button. Before, the motor buzzed quietly, like a happy little honeybee in a flower. Now it was more like a big, angry honeybee in a bottle.

"Come on! Let's ride!" said Grandpa.

I sat behind him and held on tightly around his waist.

Buuuzzz! We started slowly.

Buuuzzz! We went faster and faster.

Buuuzzz!

Soon we were racing through the park. The wind blew past me and the trees flashed by.

"This is better!" Grandpa shouted. "This is a space-age scooter. Now I will be able to visit my friends and do my shopping in style."

"Cool, Grandpa! Coooooooool!" I shouted into the wind.

Grandpa's New Scooter is a Narrative.

A narrative has an **introduction**. It tells . . .

- **who** the story is about (the characters)
- **where** the story happened
- **when** the story happened.

Introduction	
Who	
Where	
When	My dad and I visited Grandpa last weekend.

A narrative has a **problem** and a **solution**.

Problem

Solution

Guide Notes

> **Title: Grandpa's New Scooter**
> **Stage:** Fluency
>
> **Text Form:** Narrative
> **Approach:** Guided Reading
> **Processes:** Thinking Critically, Exploring Language, Processing Information
> **Written and Visual Focus:** Speech Bubbles, Thought Bubbles, Visual List

THINKING CRITICALLY
(sample questions)
- What do you think this story could be about? Look at the title and discuss.
- Look at the cover. Why do you think Grandpa needs a scooter?
- Look at pages 2 and 3. What do you think is meant by the words, *He was sitting at the table with his walking stick and a long face*?
- Look at pages 4 and 5. Why do you think a three-wheeled scooter would be better for Grandpa than Dana's scooter?
- Look at pages 6 and 7. Why do you think Grandpa wants to go faster?
- Look at pages 10 and 11. How do you know Grandpa's scooter is going to be fast?
- Look at pages 12 and 13. Why do you think Grandpa called his scooter *Fireball*?
- Look at pages 16 and 17. How do you know that Dana is enjoying her ride on Grandpa's scooter?

EXPLORING LANGUAGE

Terminology
Title, cover, illustrations, author, illustrator

Vocabulary
Clarify: walking stick, flashed, enough, streaks, groceries, space-age, borrow
Nouns: scooter, flower, trees
Verbs: blew, visit, ride, carry
Homonyms: buy/by, red/read, blew/blue
Antonyms: sitting/standing, long/short, sad/happy, strong/weak
Synonyms: happy/glad, little/small, faster/quicker
Singular/plural: battery/batteries, change/changes
Similes: and streaks *like a fireball through space*, it was more *like a big, angry honeybee in a bottle*

Print Conventions
Apostrophes – possessive (Grandpa's), contraction (let's, I'm, it's, I've)
Hyphens (three-wheeled, space-age)